Tea

A cultural history from around the world

DELICIOUS!

Ed S. Milton

Astrolog Publishing House Ltd.

Edited by: S. Milton

Cover Design: Na'ama Yaffe

Layout and Graphics: Daniel Akerman

P.O. Box 1123, Hod Hasharon 45111, Israel

Tel: 972-9-7412044

Fax: 972-9-7442714

Published by Astrolog Publishing House 2003

10 9 8 7 6 5 4 3 2 1

Red tea is a tea that has undergone a process of fermentation and is widespread mainly in China. Its caffeine content is extremely low. In England, it is customary to drink red tea with full-cream milk. Tea experts define red tea, from the point of view of its flavors, as a combination of green and black tea, but it must be remembered that the special flavor of red tea comes from the fermentation and not from the blend of two types of tea.

owadays, the English import wines from Portugal and spend their summer vacations there. However, their gratitude should be far more profound. In the 16th century, Portugal was the source from which tea reached England. Charles II married the Portuguese Catherine, a sworn aficionada of tea who introduced tea-drinking to the English royal household and to the English nobles. Two hundred years later, tea became the national drink of England.

he English concept of high tea – tea that was drunk at around four o'clock in the afternoon along with a piece of cake – stems from the English custom of eating an early luncheon and a late dinner. It is said that Anne, the Duchess of Bedford, had to allay her hunger, so she began to drink tea with a biscuit halfway between the early luncheon and the late dinner.

arl Gray, the most famous tea in the West, is a tea that is scented with bergamot oil. The name itself is the name of an English nobleman who claimed to have been given the recipe for tea during his tour of duty in China by "a member of the Chinese royal court." The fact that a popular newspaper discovered that Earl Gray had never been to China did not hinder the growing popularity of the tea that was named after him.

ea has always been considered to be a healthful beverage (as opposed to coffee, which was considered to be a "corrupting" beverage). The Chinese claim that a cup of tea stimulates keen thinking. The Japanese claim that drinking tea balances yang and yin and engenders harmony. My grandmother claims that tea soothes intestinal cramps and cures a sore throat, and when a cloth is dipped into it, it reduces swelling.

ea manufacturers will tell you at every opportunity that tea prevents and cures various diseases, mainly for one reason: tea contains anti-oxidants that neutralize the free radicals in the human body.

*I*f regular tea is healthful, green tea is really a wonder beverage. It fortifies the immune system, helps stimulate anti-aging processes, prevents symptoms of hypertension and alleviates joint inflammations.

ea plants grow in plantations and require two things: stable and very humid weather conditions and a great deal of cheap manual labor. It is no wonder that tea-growing flourished in countries where cheap labor abounds – China, India, Ceylon and Africa, for instance. Many economists claimed that tea plantations, because of the cheap work force employed in them, are a millstone around the neck of weak countries.

n India, it is believed that it was Daruma, an ascetic Indian monk who resided in China, who discovered tea in the sixth century CE. In order to prevent himself from falling asleep while deep in contemplation, the monk tore off his eyelids. The first tea plant grew in the place where his eyelids fell to the ground. When the monk tasted it, he was granted enlightenment – moreover, the beverage probably stimulated him. His followers were the first consumers of tea, and in India, tea is called "the beverage of Daruma's eyes."

or those who follow diets: tea contains no calories and it helps the digestive processes and metabolism (especially green tea). The only problem is the sugar, cream, cakes and cookies that upset the balance of the diet as a result of their close association with tea.

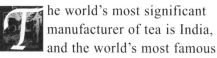he world's most significant manufacturer of tea is India, and the world's most famous tea experts are Indian. The favorite tea in India, incidentally, is "Chai Masala," which is a blend of various tea leaves and spices that are boiled together with full-cream milk.

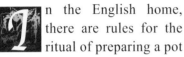n the English home, there are rules for the ritual of preparing a pot of tea. Boiling water is poured into the clean teapot and is swilled around (this stage is called "warming the teapot"). Then the water is poured out and the tea leaves – one teaspoonful per cup – are placed in the warm teapot, plus one more teaspoonful "for the pot." Boiling water is poured into the teapot, which is then covered with its lid, and exactly four minutes must elapse before the tea can be poured.

If you find it difficult to identify a teabag of good tea according to its flavor, look at the packaging! High-quality tea bags are generally made from pure silk, and they are packed in a transparent box.

he basic division of tea types is according to their color – green, black or red: green tea is not fermented, red tea is "half" fermented and black tea is fermented. The subsequent divisions are generally according to the origin of the tea leaves.

When Elizabeth I founded the East India Company in 1600, she never dreamed that the company would operate for almost 300 years and would become the biggest in the world thanks to a single product – tea! Incidentally, the East India Company was a principal player in the Boston Tea Party.

n India, tea is prepared by cooking it with milk and pouring the hot beverage into thick cups. In England, tea is prepared in a teapot and is poured into a cup containing cold milk. The difference between the customs stems from a simple reason: the expensive porcelain crockery would shatter when it came into contact with the hot beverage! In order to preserve the porcelain crockery, the English adopted the hot-onto-cold habit.

he blend of tea leaves, crop prices and rank of quality and flavors of tea are determined by professional tasters who examine tea leaves like wine – they look at them, smell them, infuse the tea and taste it. A few decades ago, the orchard owners in Ceylon claimed that the flu from which the professional taster of the East India company was suffering lowered the prices of tea and caused most of them to go bankrupt.

Turkish tea is actually a mixture of tea leaves and … an infusion of apples. The tea is sweetened with a lot of sugar, and is generally sipped from small glasses while it is very hot.

he ceremonial imbibing of tea is identified with Japan. Tea has been known in Japan since the middle of the first millennium, and was initially imported from China. In the middle of the second millennium, the growing of tea was widespread in Japan, and tea became the national drink. The Tea Ceremony is considered to be an art that reflects the Zen spirit. In this ceremony, green tea is imbibed. It is never sweetened.

*G*reen tea is tea that undergoes a process of steaming immediately after it is picked (in order to prevent fermentation), and is subsequently dried. Green tea contains only a small amount of caffeine. It is popular in China, Japan and the Arab countries, and has recently become popular in Western countries as well (because of its medicinal properties).

id you know that the teaspoon, which is used for stirring sugar into tea, originated in England 300 years ago? What's special about it is that it is bigger than a coffee spoon, so that the spoonful of sugar for tea contains about 20% more sugar than the spoonful of sugar for coffee.

All in all, tea is composed of two ingredients – leaves and… water! The Chinese and the Japanese use only pure spring water or rainwater collected in barrels for preparing tea. In the West, there is a tendency to use mineral water, and in England, water from the faucet is preferred. What they all have in common is that the water must be properly boiled before the infusion.

rab tea – sometimes known as Moroccan tea – is green tea that has been infused in a metal teapot and to which honey and mint have been added. Sometimes the tea is served without sugar, but there are sweet cookies on the tray beside it.

ecember 16, 1773 – the most famous tea party in the world took place in Boston's chilly harbor. Three hundred and forty-two tea chests heralded the tax revolt and led to the American War of Independence.

he world champion tea drinkers are... the inhabitants of the oil principalities in the Persian Gulf: 3.5 cups a day. After them come the Irish: 3 cups a day; then the English and the Chinese: 2.5 cups a day. The Indians consume only 2 cups a day, and the Iraqis only drink half a cup of tea a day on average per inhabitant!

DELICIOUS!

ugar is the main sweetener for drinking tea, and the growing and consumption of tea always heralds the growing and consumption of sugar. Since the 18th century, a vigorous dispute has raged regarding the important question: Which sugar is especially good for sweetening tea? In England, the tendency is granular sugar; in Europe, brown sugar; and in the USA, regular white sugar. In France, sugar for tea comes in the form of cubes. In Eastern Europe, it is customary to hold a sugar cube in one's mouth and suck the tea through it.

The Chinese believe that one of their emperors sat in the shade of a dense bush about 5,000 years ago sipping boiling water, as was his custom, when suddenly a fragrant leaf broke off and fell into his cup. Oblivious of this, the emperor sipped his beverage and immediately became aware of its exquisite flavor. After having beheaded the slave whose job it was to ensure that no leaves fell into his cup, the Emperor ordered the head to be wrapped in tea leaves and buried next to the plant. That was the beginning of the tea craze in China.

*T*he Japanese "Book of Tea" is famous throughout the world, but the Chinese "Book of Tea" (which was written by Lu-Yu in the eighth century) preceded the Japanese book and is in fact the first book that was ever written about the virtues of tea drinking.

he samovar is the tea-drinking center of Russia and Eastern Europe. A large container – a samovar – is heated, and at the same time a pot of strong tea essence is prepared. When people want to drink, they pour a little of the essence into a cup and add boiling water from the samovar.

hai masala, a traditional Indian tea that is often cooked in milk (instead of water), is actually a blend of three parts of tea to one part of any spice – cloves, cardamom, cinnamon and ginger.

ea leaves (and tea bags) that are not kept in an airtight container oxidize when they come into contact with the air. In the past, because of the high price of tea, tea leaves were kept in airtight, locked containers!

old tea came into being by chance. An Englishman who was exhibiting blends of tea from India and Ceylon at an exhibition in St. Louis in 1904 noticed that no one wanted to drink hot tea at the exhibition. He had a brainwave: he mixed crushed ice into the cups of tea and became the originator of cold tea.

ow we've reached black tea, which is known as "Western" tea. This tea undergoes full fermentation, oxidizes, and is then dried in hot air. Its caffeine content is high, its sugar content is minimal, and its taste is slightly "burned."

hen cultivated in plantations, the tea plants reach the height of a man at most. In most cases, they do not grow higher than five feet. When they grow wild, they can reach a height of 50 feet.

nitially, tea bags were actually commercial samples that were distributed by a tea merchant in Manhattan. The commercial sample quickly became a "hot" product. Today, some three-quarters of the tea consumed in the U.S. comes in tea bags!

The correct preparation of the blend of tea – sometimes using dozens of strains or different crops – is a very valuable trade secret. The secret of preparing a popular blend is kept behind lock and key in the same way as Coca Cola's magic formula.

*R*eading tea leaves in order to predict the future is widespread in East and West alike. Many soothsayers who use coffee grounds as well claim that tea leaves (tea leaves, not tea bags!) are especially good for predicting the future. During the reading itself, the soothsayer or medium sees various images and symbols hidden in the leaves, and uses them to interpret the character, past or future of the asker.

he following way of predicting the future with tea leaves is widespread in Arab countries:

A piece of white cotton fabric
is stretched over a wooden
frame. The asker takes a
mouthful of boiling-hot tea
(without sugar). He must
gargle three times with the tea
and then spit it out onto the
stretched fabric, forming
clumps of tea leaves in
various shapes. The reader
reads the asker's future – at
this point, the asker's mouth
is burning like hell –
according to the clumps.

he Chinese have proof that they were the first people in the world to recognize the properties of the tea plant. In a book of Chinese medicine dating from about 4,800 years ago, it is written: "This plant quenches the thirst and causes the person to be alert and not sleepy. It is good for the kidney functions and for stimulating the actions of the heart." The drink itself is described as a medicinal drink, and in another place as an elixir. In another book from the

same period, it is written: "The (tea) plant grows in the depths of winter beside streams, and is also resistant to the heaviest frost. (Its leaves) are gathered on the third day of the third month and are dried for 33 days."

hinese restaurants serve a beverage picturesquely named "Liquid Jade." Its main property is to ensure longevity. Don't get too excited – the magic drink is nothing more than (green) tea.

"Monkey's tea" in India is a magical drink. The Indians believe that the wild monkeys living in the mountains raid the tea plants that grow wild and gather their leaves. The monkeys chew the leaves and spit out the residue. Anyone who prepares tea from this masticated residue and drinks it can become an extremely powerful wizard and even make himself invisible.

*A*t least one classic work came into the world as a result of tea. Lao Tzu, who left his homeland riding on a buffalo, met Yen Hasi, the commander of a Chinese stronghold, on his way. Hasi stopped the famous sage and served him a cup of tea. As a mark of gratitude, the sage quit his wanderings and wrote the Tao Te Ching, the fundamental book of Taoism, and offered it to the commander of the fortress. Perhaps it's a better idea to call the book Tao Tea Ching?

ven though tea has been known
in different forms for
thousands of years, raising tea
plants in plantations – as opposed to
gathering tea leaves from tea plants
growing in the wild – only began in the
fourth or fifth century AD. Several
hundred years later, at the end of the
eighth century AD, the first taxes on
raising and selling tea were imposed.

u Yu, who lived in China in the eighth century, was called "The Emperor of Tea." He was a Buddhist poet who dedicated his life to writing a comprehensive work about tea. This book, "The Book of Tea," exerted a great influence on Taoist and Zen writings in the years following Lu Yu's death.

ea was widespread in Japan as early as the eighth century AD. In their palace inventories, emperors recorded gifts of "700 bags of tea that were given to 700 Buddhist monks" or "the construction of temples in each of which is a large tea garden." The tea-drinking or Chao-No-You ceremony (pouring boiling water onto tea leaves), which became an almost sacred ceremony in the 16th century, was held in a special room according to strict ceremonial rules. Nowadays, too, in Japan, one can enjoy Zen serenity and tea-drinking in special and exquisite tea rooms.

n the 15th and 16th centuries AD, European merchants, missionaries and explorers returned from voyages to the East – voyages that extended from Persia and India to China and Mongolia. Upon

their return to Europe, they brought silk, delicate porcelain and... tea. The countries that traded regularly with the East – mainly Portugal, Holland and Venice – were already familiar with the niceties of the East, but the 16th century signaled the introduction of Eastern products into Europe.

n Venice, the city council discussed the topic of Chai Catai (tea from China) in 1553, following a Persian merchant's offer of a large quantity of Chinese tea to the council. In a book dating from 1559, which was published in Venice and was actually the report of merchants' voyages, tea appears for the first time as a valuable product. It was described as "the spice of the Chinese beverage."

n 1557, the Chinese empress granted Portugal a "trade license" and a Portuguese trade center was established in Macao. During its first years, the bulk of trade involved silk and spices, but toward the end of the century, the tea trade already constituted about half of Macao's export to Europe. At the beginning of the 17th century, the Dutch began to import Japanese tea to Europe.

t the tea parties of Holland in the 17th century, it was customary to drink sweetened tea… and to smoke pipes containing tea leaves as if they were tobacco.

rom the beginning of the 16th century, tea took its place as England's national beverage. The English trade centers in the East, as well as the British East India Company, were based on trade monopolies of natural treasures such as tea, cotton or expensive wood. The English first imported Indian tea to Europe (at half the price of Chinese tea), and toward the end of the 17th century, they began to trade in Chinese tea.

ea reached Russia via Mongolia at the end of the 16th century, and, during the 17th century, directly from China, too. Caravans of hundreds of camels and thousands of horsemen-guards made their way from Mongolia to Moscow on a journey that took a year or more in order to bring cargoes of tea to Russia. The Trans-Siberian Railway, which was established in 1905, replaced the camels, and for years the bulk of its revenues derived from the transportation of tea from Mongolia to Moscow.

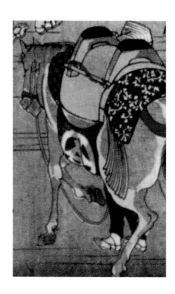

ea plants that grow in plantations or in the wild yield their most fragrant leaves at heights of 4,000 feet and above. The low temperatures at that height as well as the air with its low oxygen content cause the slow growth of the plant and the fragrance of the leaves. A trouble-free growing season in the mountain heights yields a high-quality and expensive crop. The only problem lies in the cold spells that blacken the leaves and basically disqualify them for marketing.

he tea trade enriched all the tea merchants – and impoverished the owners of the plantations and the laborers. Chinese and Indian merchants took control of the tea trade and sold tea to English companies and European merchants at twenty times the price they paid the tea growers and orchard owners. The European merchants sold the tea in Europe at a price that was twenty times what they had paid

for it. At the beginning of the 18th century, the rulers discovered the treasure they had at their fingertips, and began to impose taxes on tea growing and trading – taxes that were borne, of course, by the consumers. No wonder an English writer wrote: "In order to become wealthy in the East, all your need is a little garden of tea trees. Tea leaves are worth their weight in gold!"

n tea plantations, we actually find one type of tea plant. The differences in the quality of the crops stems not from the type of tea plant but from the weather conditions that prevailed during the growing season, and especially from the manner in which the leaves were picked and handled. Professional picking and handling of the tea leaves can treble their value as opposed to careless handling.

rom the mid-18th century until the beginning of the 20th century, experiments to grow tea in the U.S. (mainly in the South) were conducted. The main reason for the failure of these experiments was, in all cases, the low wages that were offered the laborers.

One of the reasons for the quality of the tea produced in China and Japan is the fact that tea plants grow in small plantations (in fact, tea gardens), and the plantation owner supervises the entire process during the course of his work. The quality of Chinese or Japanese tea today is considered to be superb, and the prices of the tea that comes from those places are double the prices of tea that is grown in the enormous plantations of India, Sri Lanka, Java or Sumatra. Economists dub this situation "the tea plantation paradox": the lower the wages of the laborers in the large plantations, the less money the plantation owners earn, since the price of the tea from their plantations is low.

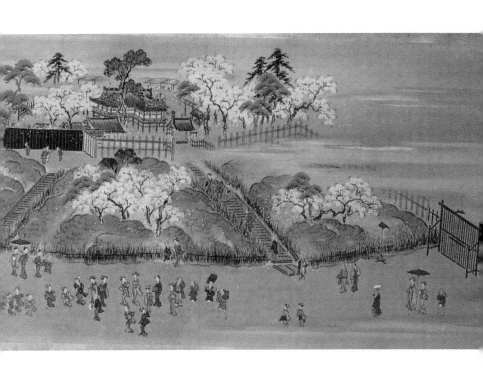

icking the leaves is generally done by women, and there is not yet any industrial substitute for manual labor. The leaves that are picked must be of the same size and moistness, otherwise the drying process is disrupted. There are tea growers who pick only the youngest leaves (2-3 leaves on each branch) and produce expensive and exclusive blends. In most cases, about 20 leaves are picked from each branch, and the regular commercial blends are produced.

ater is the most common drink in the world. Immediately after it comes tea, mainly because of the billions of heavy tea consumers in the Far Eastern countries.

n Taiwan, there is a "Tea Museum" whose uniqueness lies in presenting records regarding tea. According to this museum, the best tea in the world is Tung-Ting, which can cost up to $730 per kilogram. It grows in… Taiwan, of course.

he Chinese are more modest. According to them, the best tea is green tea, which is called "the dragon's well" after a village that is situated high in the mountains. The entire village is a living museum for the production of green tea, and visitors can see the production process of the tea and purchase a kilogram of green tea for $250.

*T*he Sri Lankans scoff at the Taiwanese and the Chinese because everyone knows that the tea produced in Sri Lanka is the best in the world. Special types of Sri Lankan tea are sold for $450 a kilogram.

n India, the prices are lower – about $150 per kilogram of high-quality tea, but the Indians claim that the tea that is grown in Bengal is the best in the world.

I myself drank a cup of tea at the Ritz Hotel in London. For a price that was equivalent to $47, I received a pot of tea (two cups), two cookies and two tiny sandwiches.

According to traditional Chinese medicine, drinking tea is effective in breaking down fats in the digestive tract and in the blood, and in inducing weight loss. Green tea is more effective than black tea. Moreover, chewing tea leaves that have been boiled in water removes fats from the skin.

andidiasis can be cured with Tea Tree Oil, which is known to be effective in the treatment of vaginal infections. A mixture of one teaspoonful of oil in one pint of boiling water is used for douching. However, don't forgo medical treatment!

roblems of athlete's foot can be solved by applying several drops of Tea Tree Oil to the infected area.

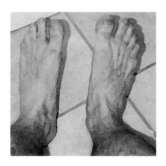

ne of the natural remedies for oral herpes is a mixture of five drops of Tea Tree Oil in a tablespoon of honey. The mixture is added to a cup of rosemary or sage tea, and gargled five times a day. A daily gargle also serves as a preventive measure against herpes.

Rum tea

For 4 servings:
4 teaspoons fresh lemon juice
120 ml rum
1 strip of lemon peel into which two cloves have been inserted
4 cups strong tea
1 cinnamon stick broken into 4 pieces

Preparation:
Mix the tea with all the other ingredients and simmer for a
minute. Serve in glasses with a piece of cinnamon stick.

Bucharian tea

For 4 servings:

2 cups water
4 tablespoons tea leaves
1 teaspoon salt
2 cups milk
1,2 or 3 teaspoons of butter
2 tablespoons chopped walnuts

Preparation:

In a pot, bring the water and tea to a boil and let it stand for a few minutes until the infusion becomes dark. Add the rest of the ingredients. Heat through and strain into cups.

Almond tea from North Africa

For 4 servings:
2 cups boiling water
1 heaped tablespoon black tea
3 tablespoons sugar
1 tablespoon water
2 tablespoons almonds
Preparation:
Combine the water and
tea into a strong, dark
infusion. Pour into
small cups. In a frying

pan, cook the sugar, the tablespoon of water and the
almonds until a dark caramel is formed, covering the
almonds. Quickly transfer the caramelized almonds
into the tea and serve.

Orange tea

For 4 servings:
2 cups boiling water
4 teaspoons tea leaves
2 cups fresh orange juice
4 teaspoons sugar
1 cup orange liqueur
4 cloves

Preparation:
Pour the boiling water over the tea leaves and let
stand for 3-4 minutes. Strain. Bring the orange juice
and sugar to the boil and stir until the sugar dissolves.
Mix the tea and the juice, add the liqueur and pour
into glasses containing one clove each.

Duck breast in orange tea

For 4 servings:
(big) whole duck breasts
2 finely chopped onions
2 cups of clear chicken broth
1or 2 cups of fresh orange juice
4 tablespoons of Earl Grey tea leaves
1 tablespoon of honey
3 tablespoons of butter
Salt and freshly ground black pepper

Preparation:

Preheat the oven to 200°C (328°F). Pierce the skin of the duck with a fork and season. Heat a heavy skillet and fry the duck breast without adding any fat (first on the skin side for about 4 minutes until golden, and then two minutes on the other side).

Transfer it to a grid in a roasting pan and roast for about 20 minutes until it is medium-rare, which is the optimal degree of cooking. You can increase the time by 2 or 3 minutes, but the duck should not be more cooked than medium.

In the fat remaining from frying the duck, fry the onion until golden. Strain and then return the onion to the skillet, add the broth, strain and squeeze the solid ingredients well in order to extract all the liquid. Add the Earl Grey tea

Return the liquid to the skillet, add honey, whisk the butter in, and season. Slice the duck breast thinly and serve hot with the sauce.

Tea bread

Ingredients:
6 cups water
6 teaspoons tea leaves or 6 teabags
1 cup golden raisins
1 cup dried cherries, stoned and chopped
1 cup sugar
1 teaspoon baking powder
1 cup light corn syrup
1 egg
2 teaspoons vanilla essence
1 cup peeled roasted pistachios

Preparation:
Boil the water and add the tea leaves. Let stand for 15 minutes.
Strain the tea and soak the raisins and the cherries in it for about an
hour. Strain and keep the liquid and the fruit.
Heat the oven to 170°C (274°F). Grease a loaf tin. Mix the flour,
sugar and baking powder and add 1 cup of the fruit liquid together
with the corn syrup, the egg and the vanilla. Knead well, preferably
with an electric mixer.
Add the dried fruit and the nuts, mix, and place the dough in the
baking tin. Back for about an hour until a toothpick comes out
clean. Invert onto a cooling rack.

ea in the ordinary sense refers to the leaves of the tea tree that have been infused in boiling water. When we infuse the leaves of other plants, fruit peels, flowers, etc. in water, we call the beverage "herbal tea."

When preparing tea, the water used in the infusion is very important. Water that has been standing in a container for a long time must not be used, nor must water that has boiled for a long time.

 f the tea leaves are infused in water for too long, the amount of tannin in the beverage increases and its taste becomes too "strong."

*I*n the Far East, it is maintained that infusing tea leaves for three minutes produces a "stimulating" beverage, while infusing tea for six minutes produces a "calming" beverage.

Herbal tea in headings:

Anise tea – effective for digestive problems and for fortifying the blood flow.

Basil tea – effective for "fortifying" the blood; helps people who suffer from low blood pressure.

Bebong tea – effective against inflammations, colds and digestive problems.

Cinnamon tea – effective against bacteria, viruses and skin fungi; lowers high blood pressure.

Clove tea – effective against toothache; is considered to be the body's "disinfectant."

Fennel tea – adds energy to the body, helps with problems in the digestive system, and helps expel fats from the body.

Laurel tea – effective for asthma sufferers.

Lavender tea – effective for people who suffer from hypertension, soothes the nerves and helps with allergy problems.

Marjoram tea – helps improve the memory.

Mint tea – effective for digestive problems; helps people who suffer from hypertension.

Nettle tea – cleanses the body of toxins.

Sage tea – effective for digestive problems and menopausal problems (both men and women).

Spearmint tea – effective for increasing the libido.

Strawberry tea – effective for inflammations in the body.

Thyme tea – effective for people who suffer from colds, stimulates the appetite and helps people who suffer from insomnia and nightmares.

Valerian tea – effective for insomniacs.

ea has an unlimited number of shapes. To be vulgar, tea can shrink and crinkle like a bad piece of material. Or it may look like the flank of an ox – some leaves sharp, some curly. It can look like a mushroom whirling around. Its leaves can swell and leap as if they were being lightly tossed on rippling water. Others will look like clay, soft and malleable, ready for the potter's touch, and will be clear and pure as if filtered through wood. Other leaves will twist and turn like rivulets made by heavy rain on freshly-tilled fields.

Those are the very finest of teas.
But there are also teas like the
husk of bamboo – with hard stems
and are too firm to steam. These are
shaped liked a sieve. There are also
those that are like a locust after a
frost – their stem and leaves are
limp, and they look like a heap of
rubble. These teas are old and
worhtless.

Lu Yu, Classic of Tea

Predicting The Future Using Tea Leaves

Foretelling the future through tea leaves - or reading the past and the present - is an ancient art form. It bears a strong resemblance to other forms of mysticism and prophecy such as palm reading, stargazing, dream interpretation, and card reading. But, there is also an essential difference.

Tea-leaf reading is very difficult to learn. In contrast to other methods of prophecy, most of whose "secrets" can be learned through courses or books, the reading of tea leaves demands a much higher degree of sensitivity and intuition - an inner force that takes over and guides the tea reader. It is very hard to teach the secret of this sensitivity or this ability to act as a medium. This is perhaps

why there are almost no basic, in-depth works devoted to the reading of tea leaves.

Why can one person read tea leaves while another sees nothing more in the leaves than dirt to be washed down the drain? To understand this, we must go back to childhood. Children like to look up at the clouds and imagine different shapes. One child will see an entire world in the clouds, while another sees nothing but the clouds themselves!

That, in a nutshell, is the difference. The tea reader does not really see anything in the usual visual sense; she sees everything solely through her inner eye. However, not everybody has the capability to be a medium. To see things in the leaves, the reader must attain a combination of euphoria and deep relaxation - a feeling of remoteness, of

floating, of slipping out of the boundaries of the body and soul. Once the reader has achieved this state, the eye itself must learn to see things, yet be detached from what it sees. As children, we would look at the clouds and say, "There's a dragon, there's a fluffy dog, there's the Eiffel Tower." All of the images were interwoven, dissolving into one another, and we would "see" an entire world. Look at the tea leaves as if they are a blue sky studded with clouds. Note the sign, the first shape that comes to mind - without trying to think about or understand it.

Following is a small selection of interpretations for predicting the future, derived from images and symbols that can be seen in the tea leaves:

Acrobat - An acrobat - a tumbler or gymnast - always symbolizes a love affair, especially if the querent is a woman. In the case of a man, the interpretation would be a love affair involving a woman connected to him. Many acrobats in one formation of tea leaves change the picture into an actual circus...or a real orgy!

Banana - The banana, due to its suggestive shape, is always associated with sex. In most cases, it is interpreted as infidelity or a significant problem (especially if the querent is a male). The precise explanation must take into account the total picture. A peeled banana indicates that the problem is getting worse.

Basket - A present awaits the seeker, or a gift that he received in the past had a practical worth far greater than its monetary value.

Bat - A significant formation. It indicates that the querent is well-schooled in disappointment, and is constantly fearful that people - even close friends - are constantly plotting against him. It is difficult to offer a possible solution. In a woman's cup, a bat also symbolizes the fear of a varied sex life, and the desperate clinging to the normal and the ordinary in her life.

Bottle - A complex shape. It indicates, first of all, health problems that endanger the individual. It can signify addiction to a substance or pastime, such as gambling, and can also point to sexual problems. It is very hard to get a precise interpretation. There is no difference between a single bottle and many bottles.

Chest - Generally appears in the form of a woman's breasts, but can also be man's chest. In any event, this formation signifies the pursuit of true love (not necessarily sexual in nature). In women, it can also indicate the desire to have a child.

Circle - A circle, which sometimes appears in the form of a ring, relates to the area of love or marriage, and appears primarily in the leaves of women. An intact circle symbolizes romantic success, marriage, reconciliation with a romantic partner, etc. A broken circle signifies problems in these same areas. A circle with a small hill in the center (resembling a breast viewed from above) means that the birth of a child, not necessarily her own, will affect the querent.

Dove - A very lucky sign! A dove is always a good formation...and unfortunately quite a rare one. A dove in the cup of a young woman about to marry is a truly outstanding sign!

Egg - A good sign. When several eggs appear together, the sign is reinforced. An egg symbolizes prosperity, success in love, a (wanted) pregnancy in the near future. Note the shapes close to the egg in order to know in which sphere the success will occur. When an unusually large egg appears in the leaves of a man or a woman, this indicates prolonged sexual frustration. A cracked or broken egg weakens the sign.

Fork - Someone close to you is betraying you. Beware of insincere speeches. (Some readers take this a step further: a fork with two tines indicates an unfaithful man, while three tines signify an unfaithful woman.)

Fountain - An excellent sign! Success, wealth and happiness in all areas of life. Boundless sexuality. Romance. A formation that is always positive.

Giant - In a man's cup, the figure of a giant indicates feelings of inferiority, whereas for a woman, it signifies prolonged sexual frustration. The giant is always measured in relation to the other formations present in the cup.

Giraffe - Impulsiveness in thought and deed leads to unexpected complications. The querent must weigh every decision carefully. Pay special attention to the position of the giraffe's head - its direction can suggest the area in which the trouble will occur. Incidentally, a giraffe adjacent to a figure with sexual significance has a different interpretation: problems in bed - and major ones!

Groom - A groom always signifies...divorce! We don't know in what way the querent will be connected with the divorce - he might be going through a divorce himself, he might be the cause of someone else's divorce, etc. - but it is clear that a divorce will affect his or her life.

Hoof - An excellent sign. A hoof protects against the evil eye and the powers of darkness. Financial success, good health, and a guarantee that the person will triumph over problems. The hoof also has meaning in a sexual context. In a woman's cup, it points to physical desires that are not being met, while for a man it indicates intense erotic urges.

Horse - The horse is a formation frequently encountered by tea readers. In principle, it is a positive figure, especially when seen to be galloping. The hindquarters of a horse may indicate that success lies beyond reach. A figure on horseback means that the querent has a loyal partner or companion. A horse's head indicates a daring love affair...or life in the shadow of danger!

Kettle - A kettle suggests minor illnesses, but also has sexual connotations (especially if the spout is visible). In the leaves of both a man and a woman, a kettle indicates sexual problems for a male, with regard to his performance and to the shape and size of his genitals.

Knife - Indicates that someone is separating the querent from his spouse or lover. This situation is virtually beyond repair.

Lemon - In a man's cup, a lemon formation indicates love of women; in a woman's cup, the lemon indicates disappointment in men.

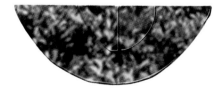

Matches -Many unsatisfying love affairs. A formation that is not flattering to the querent.

Necklace - If the necklace is whole, the querent's relationship with his or her partner is stable and positive; if it is broken, a problem is creating distance between the partners. The size of the gap between the ends indicates the extent of the problem. This is a problem that can always be solved.

Nest - A bird's nest signifies that love is the dominant factor in the querent's life. If there are eggs (or newborns) in the nest, this love is fulfilled; if there is one or more birds sitting on the nest, the love will be satisfied in the near future. An empty nest can indicate a love that no longer exists.

Nose - A nose indicates that something has taken place without the knowledge of the querent - right under his nose.

The precise interpretation depends on the adjacent shapes and on the direction in which the nose is pointing. Many tea-leaf readers give the nose a sexual significance - the size of the nose indicating the severity of the problem.

Octopus - An octopus, taken by itself, is a bad sign. It tells the person that he must seek the help of others in solving his problems. Interestingly enough, the sexual interpretation is unhappiness at the absence of a meaningful relationship, for a woman; or serious problems involving sexual expression, for a man. Incidentally, in the leaves of children, or that refer to children, an octopus indicates repressed fears or severe traumas. It is important to look into this!

Onion - An onion shows that the person is hiding something from his or her partner that is significant enough to hurt that person. A common formation. Certain tea readers claim that an onion shape in a woman's cup indicates feelings of guilt over having aborted or prevented a pregnancy in her past.

Package - A common formation. A package generally indicates a surprise for the querent in the near future. We do not know exactly what kind of surprise - it is very difficult to give either a positive or a negative interpretation. A different explanation, in the case of a man asking about a woman, relates to the package's presentation: a package that is tied up signifies an upright woman, even a virgin, whereas an open package suggests a woman with hidden sexual urges.

Person - A formation in the shape of a person is one of the hardest signs to interpret. The figure itself can take several different forms: a man or a woman, an old person or a child. We tend to interpret male or female figures in the contexts of love, sex, marriage or divorce - male-female relationships - while the interpretations of figures of children or old people focus mainly on health.

When the querent is a man, figures of a woman or women indicate sexual or romantic ties. The tea reader must interpret the figures and their status carefully, based on other formations. If only male figures are present in a male querent's cup, we can deduce that he has homosexual tendencies - or that he is a cuckold. The presence of many female figures indicates that he is a Casanova. Since several figures, of both sexes, often appear in tea leaves, you must steer your way carefully among the various interpretations.

When the querent is a woman, the basic principle is the same. If only female figures appear in the leaves, either she has lesbian tendencies or women have had an inordinate influence in her life. Numerous male figures mean that she is a flirt. A lone male figure signifies the one great love of her life!

The presence of many figures complicates the picture. If, for example, in a man's cup, we see the figures of a man and a woman, this may mean that his lover is having an affair on the side...or that his parents had a decisive influence on his life. So, much caution is needed here!

The interpretation of human figures is a rather advanced stage of tea reading, and requires much experience. As a rule, the reader should first interpret all the symbols that appear in the leaves, and only then look at the human figures. Be extremely cautious!

Pineapple - A pineapple signifies that the person is involved in many arguments and minor disputes, but also tends to seek reconciliation and compromise with his opponents after every quarrel. When the querent is a woman, a pineapple indicates the presence of many suitors or lovers in her life.

Ring - In general, a ring signifies marriage. If the ring is whole, a marriage will take place shortly, or the future of an existing marriage is assured. A broken ring indicates marital problems, but not necessarily divorce. A ring can appear in the tea leaves of married people, without the marriage or divorce being directly related to the querent. A ring also signifies the pursuit of spiritual enlightenment.

Snail - An interesting formation. A snail generally denotes a passionate, uninhibited sexual nature. A mysterious figure, most of which lies hidden.

Stork - In a woman's cup, a stork indicates virginity, lack of sexual experience - to the point where the querent may even be bothered by it. There is also a connection between the stork and pregnancy or childbirth. A stork with a broken wing in a woman's cup, she does not wish to be pregnant. A stork in a man's cup indicates that he has a fertility problem.

Tiger - A formation that indicates a spirit of adventure, flightiness. In a man's tea leaves, it also signifies a cruel streak, while for a woman, it points to brazen sexuality.

Tree - A good sign. The person will succeed and flourish, without losing touch with reality. Also a positive symbol for a man or woman suffering from sexual problems: a tree indicates that the solution is close at hand.

Vine - A vine, which usually appears bearing clusters of grapes, is interpreted differently for a man and a woman. When it appears in a man's cup, it is a sign of financial success; in a woman's cup, the interpretation is completely different - sexual problems and inhibitions, lack of sexual satisfaction.

Witch - A common formation. Always signifies another woman who has a significant influence on the querent - male or female. It is important to understand that a witch is not necessarily an evil woman. In the cup of a married woman, for example, a witch can symbolize her husband's lover! In a man's cup, this figure often represents his mother-in-law. The formation is interpreted with the help of adjacent shapes.

Zipper - A difficult formation. A zipper indicates impotence (even when it appears in a woman's cup, in which case it refers to the man in her life). This is a formation without an answer - we cannot find a reason or a solution in the tea leaves.

Coffee

A cultural history from around the world

Ed S. Milton

9654941589

Tea

A cultural history from around the world

Ed S. Milton

9654941597

Olive Oil

A cultural history from around the world

Ed S. Milton

9654941600

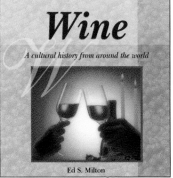

Wine

A cultural history from around the world

Ed S. Milton

9654941619